THE LORD'S PRAYER

ANTONIO GENTILE
ALBERTO CAMICI

The Lord's Prayer

ST PAULS

Original title: *Padre nostro (Mistagogia della preghiera del Signore)*
© 1994 Editrice Ancora, Milan, Italy

Translated by Sr Frances Teresa OSC

Cover illustration: Painting from the Catacomb of St Callistus, reproduction used by kind permission of Edizioni San Paolo s.r.l., Italy
Drawings by Enrico Sironi

ST PAULS
Middlegreen, Slough, SL3 6BT, United Kingdom
Moyglare Road, Maynooth, Co. Kildare, Ireland

English translation © ST PAULS (UK) 1995

ISBN 085439 510 5

Set by TuKan, High Wycombe
Printed by Biddles Ltd, Guildford

ST PAULS is an activity of the priests and brothers of the Society of St Paul who proclaim the Gospel through the media of social communication

Contents

THE OUR FATHER
A PRAYER TO BE OWNED,
REALIZED AND LIVED

Who could count the pages and books dedicated to the Our Father? They range from Tertullian, the first of the Fathers to comment on it, to the *Catechism of the Catholic Church*. Yet why is it that so many writers through the centuries have felt this need to explain the prayer of Jesus? Why is there always room for further commentaries to help us understand it?

In the end, it is the nature of the Our Father itself which demands this, because it is so concentrated a prayer.

The Our Father, a concentrated formula

The horizons of the Our Father are limitless. Beneath its short phrases flows all the prayer of scripture as well as all the religious experience of Jesus and the first Christian communities. In Tertullian's famous expression, the Our Father is a "compendium of the whole Gospel", which is why the Church has always seen it as a summary, guide and frame of reference for all Christian prayer. In addition to this, all the life and experience of human history are condensed in the Lord's Prayer, all humanity's struggling development, all our deep problems, our need for faith, for bread and for forgiveness.

A familiar prayer, ever to be discovered

The Our Father is only a few lines, yet it can be repeated endlessly, learnt by heart, and always bring fresh discoveries. Its phrases are short, its words simple, its depths immense.

All our reflection and study are needed, but these are not enough. The only interior guide who can lead us into the mystery of the Our Father is the Spirit of the Lord whom we invoke in faith. Because the Our Father is open-ended, it is a prayer for a life-time. Our understanding of it never ceases to mature and the lessons in living which it gives us are never finished. Its meaning and importance reveal themselves to us more and more. Through daily hearing and meditating on the word of God, through the experiences of our lives with all their problems and sufferings, through our constant prayer and our growing imitation of Jesus, the petitions of the Our Father are illumined for us.

A cultural and living understanding

In so far as it is a concentrated formula, therefore, the Our Father needs some explanation so that we can bring the meaning of its short petitions into our lives. Prayer is a human act, not just the repetition of words, so we must pray with our minds, savouring that which we say. We must bring to the text both our reflection and the understanding of our minds, for both are necessary if we are to integrate the prayer into the rich and complex dynamic of our being.

The human being is an incarnate spirit, a social person, and we cannot keep any of our attitudes entirely locked up within ourselves. It is the same with prayer. Prayer is rooted in our hearts, but its full flowering, is in the sound of words, in writings, in action... It also becomes a formula, a ritual.

A symphony to be repeatedly performed

To be sure, the formula is not the prayer, just as the score is not the music. Yet the formula is as necessary to the prayer as the score to music. The formula codifies religious experience and passes it on to others. So with the Our Father. This prayer of Jesus is like the score in which his words, like notes in music, develop the most wonderful symphony of love for the Father and for us.

As the creative playing of a symphonic score gives us living music, so the words of the Our Father, when they are not just repeated like a dead letter but prayed from the heart, give us the Son's living and loving dialogue with the Father. The words becomes a school of faith and prayer for us.

Creative repetition as a school of prayer

A child learns to speak by repeating the words he hears. However much he mangles them, he is learning through repetition to adapt the words to his capacity, and by the strength of this repetition it one day happens that the word in all its clarity and perfection flowers on his lips. In faith, a Christian is always a small child, inexpert in speaking with God. We need to learn to pray and we begin by repetition. We recite, almost stutteringly, the words which Jesus places on our lips in the Our Father.

We must also involve ourselves in this repetition, cleaving with all our being to the words on our lips and in our minds. This is creative repetition, through which we make the words our own. Understanding them, we take them into ourselves and we bring them into play in the actual (and always unpredictable) situations of our lives and so they gradually acquire new and richer meanings. They also become an examination of conscience and a teaching about how we are to live.

Human words are both as fragile as a breath and as powerful as a fulcrum or a weapon. A word is never neutral or indifferent because a good word always carries a positive charge. Such a good word would be that of a prayer like the Our Father when it is not just recited but truly

9

prayed. Its words then are revelation, bringing us to awareness, generating thoughts, feelings and decisions within us. They are a school of prayer.

The Our Father, the Christian prayer

The words of the Our Father are not simply human words, but they are the true words of God in human form. This means that they have divine efficacy, we might even dare to say that when they are said in Jesus and with Jesus, they are almost sacramental. It is this which gives them that specific character, this is the novelty of Christian prayer. Christian prayer depends on two things. The first is the coming into the world of Jesus, the Son of God, and the mystery of his incarnation, passion, death and resurrection. The other is baptism, which inserts us into that paschal mystery. The Christian prays in Jesus and Jesus prays in us. We share in Jesus' prayer. He has not only taught us the Our Father but has also experienced it in its every invocation.

Paraphrasing Paul who said: It is no longer I who live but Christ who lives in me (Gal 2:20), the Christian can truly say: It is no longer I who pray but Christ who prays in me. When we pray, we call God our Father more truly, for we are God's children from the moment when, through baptism in him, Jesus and the Spirit of Jesus are present in us.

For the Christian, the sacraments, especially our sharing in the Eucharist, are the main pillar of our prayer. This sacramental communion is the pillar of pillars. Through it, we truly become one being with Jesus. In him and with him, we can pray to the Father as at no other moment. This is why the Eucharist is the "locus" of the Our Father and why the Church puts this prayer on the lips of the faithful before they receive this sacramental communion.

The Our Father: a guide book for initiation

All we have touched upon is developed in this present work which is so rich, biblically and liturgically. It is a true guide in how to make the prayer of Jesus our own, how to make it real in our lives.

The first two chapters answer the need for a genuinely biblical understanding of the Our Father. The invocations of the Lord's Prayer are considered within the context of the Gospel and Jesus' life, above all of his passion. Here we most clearly see the full Christological dimension of the prayer and that this cannot be separated from the dimension of eschatology. This means that the incarnate Christ, who died and rose again, whom we "re-member", is also the Christ of the future before whom we stand and whose coming we await. The words of the prayer draw all their relevance from the light of Christ's glory as he lives with the Father. As we journey to meet him, it is he who illumines our prayer and gives it meaning.

The last three chapters develop the Our Father very concretely and practically, as a prayer of teaching and initiation. The journey of initiation and the way in which we make this prayer our own comes to involve our whole selves, all our nature as incarnate spirits. This means our minds and hearts, our bodies and their living rhythms, ranging from our breath itself to the full variety and richness of bodily gesture.

The dimension of the Our Father which we might call liturgical indicates more than the reflections and proposals of the rite of *traditio*. Rather, it is the driving force of the whole book. Apart from the fact that this prayer is precious to every disciple of Jesus, the book is useful and handy for everyone, from the pastoral worker to the catechist. In fact, catechesis, as we love to say, is either education in prayer or it is not catechesis. Here we would add that there can be no catechesis in prayer without a true initiation into the Our Father.

The Our Father: a programme for life

We conclude by recalling that while the Our Father is indeed a prayer-formula to be recited faithfully, it is more than that. It needs to be lived and experienced, it is both prayer and a programme for life. Its words must not only reach our hearts but also our actions. We are called to commit ourselves to live that which we ask for from the Father in our prayer.

If this is lacking, and the words we speak are not happening more and more in the way we live, then there is little point in the effort to understand and make those words our own. When this is happening, however, then the Our Father comes into its own. It becomes a school of prayer and Christian living. Such schooling is never done in this life, it will only end when we see face to face the one whom we have never ceased to call upon in faith even while we see nothing.

* * *

Part One

THE OUR FATHER
INITIATION INTO PRAYER,
PRAYER OF INITIATION

The title of this first part of our search is not just a play on words. This becomes clear as soon as we realize that the Our Father is *par excellence* the initiation into Christian prayer. The Our Father is also an initiation into prayer in the sense that it introduces the praying believer into the mysteries of God.

The Our Father "is the guide through which the primitive Church, and the Church today, initiates the catechumens into the practice of prayer. Once the catechumens have become children of God, then and now, they recite the Our Father out loud during the Eucharistic celebration. This is an immediate preparation for communion. So the Our Father is their first stumbling word of Christian prayer, their first prayer. From then on, it will be a light to them all through their lives, a strong *vademecum* for their devotion. There is no doubt but that this prayer of the Lord has been, and still is, the primary prayer of the universal community of those who believe in Christ. It is the paradigm of Christian ecumenism, an intimate link binding all the Christian churches and therefore it is a solid basis from which to seek the desired unity. Then it can become a shared point of departure in that daily dialogue between the Church and all those who believe in the one God, calling upon him as Father."[1]

For almost two thousand years, exegesis, spirituality and catechesis have each in turn thrown light upon the unfathomable riches of the Lord's prayer, deepening our understanding of it. For this reason, we would wish libraries to have a whole section reserved for the most significant texts on the Our Father.[2]

It is indicative that Christ opened his school of prayer by teaching us the Our Father and that so many Christian authors, beginning with the Fathers of the Church, have made it their starting point. They found it an essential prayer, and used it as a preliminary for all their own instructions on prayer. In spite of this, we must admit that often the Our Father is for us, both individually and collectively, little more than a rather wordy vocal prayer. Yet this is exactly what Christ spoke against, placing his own style of praying in opposition to verbosity (cf Mt 6:7-8a). Nor must we forget that when Christ exhorted his disciples to pray the Our Father, he told them to go into their own rooms (cf Mt 6:6), as if he were saying that the dimensions of community and of the personal must meet in our one life and be part of our one growth in experience of the Father.

Yet in spite of the wishes of Christ, we have, for the most part, reduced the Our Father to a formula, exactly what he wanted to avoid. The speed and volume of our recitation and the lack of recollection in our minds, empties it of all that capacity to initiate which is its particular gift. Indeed the Our Father is not really a text to recite but a series of summons, drawing God's own thoughts out of our hearts and preparing us to receive God's gifts. Saint Teresa of Jesus understood this very well when she said: "It is better to say a single word of the Our Father from time to time, than to recite the entire prayer a number of times but in haste".[3] More recently, someone has said that to recite the Our Father well, we should take at least five minutes over it (I. Dragicevic). Another has said that the Our Father will yield up all its riches when we give a whole hour to the silent saying of it (A. Gasparino).

All this bears out what we said at the start: the Our Father is not only the supreme initiation into prayer, but it is also the most excellent prayer of Christian initiation.[4]

THE GIVING OF THE OUR FATHER

In the first centuries of the Church, the giving (in Latin: *traditio*) of the Our Father was a decisive moment in the Christian initiation of those preparing for baptism. The old *Ordines Romani* show that this took place after the Creed and in the way we shall describe. First let us note that, as the ancient catechesis indicates, a correct recitation by the community meant a pause between each invocation to allow deep interior echoes to surface in response to the Lord's words.

After the *Redditio Symboli* or the giving of the Apostles' Creed, including the recitation of the Creed by the catechumens, came the *traditio orationis Dominicae*, the handing over of the Lord's Prayer. It was done in this way:

After the recitation of the Creed, the deacon says:

Stand in silence, listen with attention.

The priest then expounds the Lord's Prayer:

Our Lord and Saviour Jesus Christ, among the other precepts of salvation, gave this formula of prayer to his disciples when they asked him how to pray. The present instruction will now make it known to you as well. Let your love, then, listen to the way he taught his disciples to pray to God, the almighty Father: Whenever you pray, go into your room and shut the door and pray to your Father (Mt 6:6). This room he mentions does not mean a retired corner of the house, but that we withdraw

17

into the secrecy of our hearts, which are laid bare before God alone. To adore God with the door shut means that with a mystic key we must close our hearts to every sinful thought. With our lips closed, let us then speak to God in purity of spirit, then our God will hear our faith better than our voice. The key of faith closes our hearts against every snare of the adversary. Let it open only for God, recognising that we are his temple, for God dwells in our hearts. Let him be the advocate of our prayer. He who is the Word of God, the Wisdom of God, Christ our Lord, has taught us this prayer and so we pray in this way:

Then the priest comments on the Our Father:

OUR FATHER IN HEAVEN: This is a cry of freedom, filled with faith. According to these words, you must live in such a way that you can indeed be children of God, brothers and sisters of Jesus Christ. How would we dare call God our Father unless we do the will of God? So, beloved, show yourselves worthy of this divine adoption because it is written: To all who believed in him, he gave power to become children of God.

HALLOWED BE YOUR NAME: This does not mean that God is made holy through our prayers, for God is always holy. We are asking that his name be made holy in us, that as we have been sanctified in baptism, so may we persevere in that which we have already begun to be.

YOUR KINGDOM COME: In reality, when does God not rule, for his kingdom is everlasting? By saying: Your kingdom come, we are asking that our kingdom may come, the kingdom of God's promise which has been won by the blood and suffering of Christ.

YOUR WILL BE DONE: May God's will be done in this

way: that as God wills in heaven may we, dwellers on the earth, fulfil it without fault.

GIVE US THIS DAY OUR DAILY BREAD: We must understand here that we are speaking of spiritual food. Our bread is Christ, who said of himself: I am the bread of life come down from heaven. We ask for this bread daily because we always seek to be preserved from sin and worthy of this bread from heaven.

FORGIVE US OUR TRESPASSES AS WE FORGIVE THOSE WHO TRESPASS AGAINST US: This precept shows that we do not deserve forgiveness for our own sins unless we have first forgiven those who have offended us. As the Lord said in the Gospel: If you don't forgive others their sins, neither will your heavenly Father forgive you yours.

AND LEAD US NOT INTO TEMPTATION: This does not mean that we shall not be troubled by the tempter, the author of corruption. Scripture says: God tempts no-one to do evil. The tempter is the devil and in order to overcome him, the Lord has told us: Watch and pray lest you fall into temptation.

BUT DELIVER US FROM EVIL: This is why the Apostle said: You do not know what you should ask for in prayer. We must so pray to the one, almighty God, that in mercy we shall not be overcome in the struggle against all that which human weakness can neither resist nor flee. This victory is won by our Lord Jesus Christ, our God, who lives and reigns in the unity of the Holy Spirit, for ever and ever.

After this exposition, the deacon gives the following admonition:

Remain in silence, listen with attention.

19

The priest then says:

You have heard, beloved, the holy mysteries of the Lord's Prayer. Go now and meditate on them in your heart so that you may be made perfect in Christ and by your prayer be granted the mercy of God. The Lord our God has the power both to lead you who run in faith to the bath of regeneration, and also to unite you with himself in the kingdom of heaven. Therefore we pass on to you the mystery of the Catholic faith. He lives and reigns with God the Father in the unity of the Holy Spirit, for ever and ever. Amen.[5]

Inspired by these pages, how much more ready are they then for the so-called "mystagogy",[6] the actual period of initiation into the Christian mystery. This is included in the celebration of the Word as a preparation for the Lord's Prayer. There are now movements within the Church which, in preparing catechumens for baptism, set out to travel this road of Christian initiation, and it is encouraging to see that these have already been given a place in the praxis of the Church.[7]

An ancient ritual restated for today

In the following pages, we will consider the giving of the Our Father during the Mass. This could well happen on a Sunday, since it is better for it to be celebrated in the presence of the parish who are all making this journey together. It could take place at a time of retreat or during a period like Advent or Lent. As we are recalling the journey of the Christian life, already begun in baptism and including the other sacraments of Christian initiation, it is particularly appropriate for the celebration to take place with a liturgical group or a prayer group.

The celebration focuses around the giving of the Our Father. This is repeated phrase by phrase in the form of a dialogue between priest and the whole assembly. It is then given in written form, so that it can be a daily sign, reminding them of their responsibility for personal daily prayer as well as of their education in the faith.

Entry procession

Those concerned process in carrying lighted candles, and go to their places. Mass begins and after a homily, or admonition from the celebrant, continues until after the Gospel.

Presentation

When the Gospel has been read, there follows the presentation by the catechist or a representative of the community, who says:

Reverend Father, thanks to the Lord and through the work which God has begun in these our brothers and sisters, we ask that the prayer of the Lord be shared with them. Then, taught by the word of Jesus and enlightened by the practice of both public and private prayer, they may come to a more perfect understanding of spiritual things and to the fullness of life in Christ.

Homily

Renewal of baptismal promises (with lighted candles)

Prayer of the faithful (with the particular intention of those who are receiving this deeper initiation into their journey)

Mass continues with the Eucharistic prayer.

Giving of the Our Father

The Canon of the Mass ends with the singing of the doxology. The priest then listens to the request which is made by one of the group in the name of all.

Reverend Father, the apostles asked the Master to teach them to pray, for they wondered at his own continual, filial and often solitary prayer. The Lord replied: When you pray, say Our Father.

Today we, too, coming together in the presence of the risen Lord, want to make the same request: Teach us to pray!

Therefore we ask you to teach us to pray the Our Father, as the Church has learnt it from the Lord and now has the task of teaching it to others.

The priest responds by reciting the Our Father phrase by phrase and the whole assembly repeat it after him calmly and without shouting. It would seem helpful, after an explanation, to accompany the words with the gesture of extending the arms out. The prayer goes like this:

- Our Father in heaven
- hallowed be your name
- your kingdom come
- your will be done
  on earth as it is in heaven.
- Give us this day our daily bread
- and forgive us our trespasses
  as we forgive those who trespass against us
- and lead us not into temptation,
  but deliver us from evil.

Mass proceeds with the rite of communion.

After the final prayer but before the blessing and dismissal, the priest gives the written Our Father to each member of the group. As he does so, he says:

(Name) receive the Lord's prayer.
The daily saying of this prayer and the deeper understanding of its meaning, will give you the mind of
Christ himself and make you grow in communion and
knowledge of God.

All reply: Amen.

THE OUR FATHER
A COMPENDIUM OF THE WHOLE GOSPEL

"The Our Father, being the prayer of the Father's children, was taught by the Son of the Father to his disciples. It is a perfect synthesis of his message and a faithful expression of his inner life. It contains 'all the essentials of our prayer'" (Cyprian). More than that, it is not only the "pattern for our desires" (Augustine) but also "a precious synthesis of prayer and of the way in which we should pray" (*Roman Catechism*). "In the Our Father, Jesus has condensed the essentials of all Christian aspiration" (Van den Bussche). It contains within itself "the whole of contemplation and perfection [...] the entire spiritual way" of the believer (Teresa of Jesus). Those who are on this way see in the Our Father a model of prayer (Van Dyke) for the Christian; it is prayer *par excellence* for the Church (Bonhoeffer). More than that, the Our Father is, strictly speaking, the Christian faith made prayer. This was how it was understood by its first commentator who defined it as a compendium of the whole Gospel (Tertullian), and modern exegetes fully agree with this. They see in it the nucleus of prayer, and at the same time, the key which opens prayer up to us (Schurmann). Its best commentary is the "life, death and resurrection of him who taught it to us" (Manson).[8]

This collection of thoughts explains why the Our Father is usually preceded by an admonition and followed by the "embolism" as it is called, the concluding doxology "for yours is the kingdom, the power and the glory now and for ever" (*Didache* and *Apostolic Constitution*). These help to underline the exceptional nature of this prayer, which stands at the peak of human communication with the divine. It is the *parrhesia* or evangelical audacity of children who "dare to say". In its three articles on the Our Father, the *New Catechism of the Catholic Church*, in line with tradition and the *Roman catechism*, gives a note on the embolism. This underlines the doxological character of the first three invocations and the aspect of supplication in the last three. Both are intrinsic to the pilgrim life of the Christian.

The best way of saying the Our Father is to make it the prayer of our hearts. This is clearly what Christ wanted when he taught us to go into our rooms and close the door when we are going to pray. What is the purpose of this if not to bring us, as far as possible, into the mind and heart of Jesus as he prayed this prayer, thoughts and feelings which his disciples then made their own?

Saint Ignatius noticed that when we say a prayer like the Our Father or the Hail Mary, that it is important and fruitful of grace to unite ourselves with those in heaven, to "say it as they would say it!".[9] Similarly, it can help us if we seek out all the parallels in the Gospel between the words of the Our Father and the other words of Christ. This would be the best possible preliminary exercise before praying the Our Father. It could be done in a small group or as part of some spiritual exercises, and could proceed in this way: the guide formulates each invocation, followed by a pause. Then all those present are invited to share whatever has arisen spontaneously within them, what that phrase has evoked in them. This can be in their own words or in those of Scripture. Said in this way by a group who are able to share, the Our Father can easily extend for as long as half an hour.

Although we have anticipated in some respects, let us now move on to the practice strictly so-called. One preliminary exercise of a catechetical nature, would be to ask ourselves: what does each expression of the Our Father say to me? What thoughts and feelings does it invoke in me? To use this approach at the beginning helps us understand the basis from which we are operating. The *Catechism*[10] highlights that we might find an obstacle in the very first word: Father, unless we purify our hearts from "paternal and maternal images, stemming from our personal and cultural history, and influencing our relationship with God" (n. 2779). Something similar could be said about all the other key words of the Lord's Prayer, such as name, kingdom, will, bread, forgive, temptation, the Evil One.

In the second place, but always within the catechetical context, we might ask what echoes we spontaneously notice, between Scripture and the text of the Our Father. At this point, let us offer some specific exercises.

Exercise 1:
Lips-mind-heart and inner echoes

We place ourselves in a prayerful frame of mind, making sure that we have quiet of body and recollection of spirit. We turn towards the Father with the words and, still more, the feelings, of Christ. These the Spirit will suggest to us through the groanings within our heart of Abba-Father. The Our Father leads us deep into the heart of the Trinity.

We energize those three centres through which the word of the Lord will pass. These are the same centres which we mark with the sign of the cross when the Gospel is read, in order to consecrate them for receiving and witnessing to the Good News. Our *lips* pronounce the words of Christ; our *mind*s translate them into deep and powerful thoughts, as if they were being carved before our eyes; our *heart*s gather and register every inner vibration, sometimes many a second, as we say: Father; name; kingdom; will, or bread; forgive; deliver. Thus we read in Psalm 19:15: "You have accepted the words of my lips, before you is the trembling of my heart" (literally!).

We pause between the invocations to assist this process of taking the word into ourselves, to give a personal dimension to this transition from lips to mind and heart. If we become distracted, we only need to pick up at the point where we left off, or the point which the group has now reached, as if our prayer had only begun at that moment. We do this without impatience or fuss. Even if we have really only attended to one of the invocations of the Our Father, we have still prayed well.

After some such introduction, we might proceed in the following way. Let the guide say: Our Father who are in heaven; and the group repeat it after him. Then have a silent pause which can go on for as long as needed for the invocation to echo in the mind and heart. It is as if, after saying it with the lips, we opened an imaginary mouth in our foreheads and then in our breasts, in order to repeat the words of the Lord there too. Then the guide introduces the next invocation saying: Father, hallowed... Thus the group proceeds from one invocation to the other: Hallowed be your name; Your kingdom come; Your will be done; and so on until the end.

At the end of the prayer, take a final pause to allow that invocation of the seven which has most spoken to us, to reverberate within us. Let the invocation be as if sculptured on our hearts. This prayer will endure because it is bound to an expression/thought/feeling which is rooted deep within us.

Everyone might then say aloud which invocation has most struck their souls. Allow a short interval between people, so that each may make the invocation their own, repeating it interiorly with the inflections of the voice they have just heard.

Exercise 2:
Gospel echoes

This exercise considers two different modes. Proceed as for Exercise 1. The guide of the prayer speaks into the pause after each invocation, offering a short Gospel text. This will throw light on the feelings of Christ in the invocation (left-hand column), or on the feelings which the Lord's

Prayer is here designed to awaken in the disciples (right-hand column). We offer a brief example.[11] The numbers indicate the seven invocations of the Our Father.

Did you not know that I must be about my Father's business?	1	There is one who is your Father, he who is in heaven and you are all brothers
I have glorified you on earth, I have done the works which you gave me to do.	2	Men shall see your good works and glorify your Father who is in heaven
Blessed is he who comes in the name of the Lord. Blessed is the coming kingdom of God	3	The kingdom of God is not here nor there, but within you
My meat is to do the will of the one who sent me	4	Not everyone who says Lord, Lord, will enter the kingdom of heaven, but the one who does the will of my Father who is in heaven
I am the bread that has come down from heaven to give life to the world	5	He who eats me, lives by me
The Son of Man is come to seek and to save that which was lost	6	If your brother sin against you, forgive him. And if he sin seven times a day, forgive him
Now is the hour of darkness, but the Prince of this world will be overcome	7	Holy Father, I do not ask you to take them out of the world, but to deliver them from the Evil One

This way of praying the Our Father can be extended in a community context as we have said above.

Exercise 3:
Echoes with the Apocalypse

We offer here, by way of meditation, as much as has been written about the rapport between the Apocalypse and the Our Father.

The Apocalypse is an eschatological commentary on the Lord's Prayer. The sanctification, hallowing, of the divine name is found in every hymn throughout the book. The intercession about the kingdom coming fills the heart of the seer. The rule of the third invocation, according to which that order which obtains in heaven must also hold sway here on earth, is the motive force of the whole text. The final and decisive will of God is that the world be saved. The asking for daily bread ends, eschatologically, with the wedding feast of the Lamb (19:7-9); that of forgiving our sins in the adorning of the Bride, clothed with innocence, washed in the blood of the Lamb (7:1-7; 19:8). If we pray that the Church may be preserved and saved from final tribulation, God hears this desire, placing his seal on the Church and drawing her to himself (7:1-7; 14:1-5).[12]

Exercise 4:
The Our Father and Our Lady

Still in a biblical key, we can deepen our recitation of the Our Father by the loving experience of Mary. Let us look at each invocation:

1. *Our Father*...: "Mary, the predestined and firstborn daughter of the Father"[13] is venerated in the eastern tradition as *teonimpha*, the bride of God. At the moment of the annunciation, she became the first creature to whom the secrets of Trinitarian life were disclosed.[14]

2. ... *Name*: According to Lk 1:31, Mary was the first to know the human name of God: Jesus. In her *Magnificat* she proclaims his holy name (Lk 1:49).

29

3. ... *Kingdom*: The angel announced to Mary that the kingdom of her Son would know no end (Lk 1:33). She, in her turn, is called Queen.

4. ... *Will*: Mary said: let it be done unto me as you have said (Lk 1:38). At Cana she recommended: Do whatever he tells you (Jn 2:5). She herself was numbered among those who heard the word of God and kept it (cf Lk 11:28).

5. ... *Bread*: The Virgin has been called the Mother of the Eucharist[15] in that it was she who first gave her body and thus gave us the body of Christ. Mystical tradition finds an intimate link between Mary and the Eucharist, because the reception of the Bread from heaven leads us into a process of spiritual begetting.

6. ... *Forgiveness of sins*: Mary is full of grace (Lk 1:28) and Jesus her Son will save his people from their sins (Mt 1:21).

7. ... *Temptation/the Evil One*: Mary confronted much hardship during her life, even though she was freed from any slavery to evil. The Apocalypse sketches in the presence of the woman clothed with the sun whom Satan attempts to entrap but who emerges with total victory (cf Apoc 12:1ff; Gen 3:15).

NOTES TO PART ONE

1. S. Sabugal, *Il Padre nostro nella catechesi antica e moderna*, Palermo 1988, pp. 15-16.
2. Sabugal, in the work already quoted, offers us a representative bibliography of such works, including Cyprian, Origen, Cyril of Jerusalem, Gregory Nazianzen, Ambrose, Chrysostom, Augustine, Teresa of Avila, The Roman Catechism, Bonhoeffer and van den Bussche, as well as Sabugal himself.
3. Teresa of Jesus, *The Way of Perfection* 31,13.
4. For the convenience of our readers, we can anticipate certain texts by referring to the following: S. Weil, *Waiting on God*; O. Baumer Despeigne, *Il Pater noster come cammino iniziatico*, in "Quaderni del Centro interreligioso H. Le Saux" 4 (1983) 93-106; M. Ledrus *Il Padre nostro preghiera evangelica*, Rome 1981; Michaëlle, *Le pélerin danseur. Eveil intérieur et pédagogie du geste*, Paris 1978, pp. 120-26; K. McAll, *Healing the Family Tree*, London 1993, pp. 143-163; R. Steiner, *Il*

Padre nostro, una considerazione esoterica, Milan 1980; O. Clément –
B. Standaert, *Pregare il Padre nostro*, Bose 1988.

5. E. Lodi, *Liturgia della Chiesa,* Bologna 1981, pp 691-693.

6. Mystagogy comes from *mysterion* and *ago* (I lead) and is best expressed by the concept of initiation into mystery. This can either mean that act by which someone is led into a living understanding of revelation as Word and Sacrament (the mystagogy); or the developing personal understanding on the part of the one being initiated. The reality and the importance of mystagogy as a fundamental aspect of Christian experience has been thrown into relief by the Synod of Bishops 1985, which spoke of that 'Christian mystagogy' which becomes 'a pathway of introduction to the life of the liturgy'. (Final report B/2 in *Enchiridion vaticanum* 9/1799. Cf J. Castellano Cervera, *Pedagogia della preghiera. Mistagogia pastorale dell'orazione personale e comunitaria*, Rome 1993.) Further information can be found in A. Gentili, *Dentro il mistero*, Milan 1993.

7. RCIA, *The Rite of Christian Initiation of Adults*, 1984.

8. Sabugal, *Il Padre nostro nella catechesi...* cit., pp. 19-20.

9. *Spiritual Exercises*, n. 248.

10. As is well known, the *Catechism of the Catholic Church*, 1992, concludes with a long section on the Our Father (nn. 2759-2865). This prayer of Jesus is the ABC of Christianity. By way of commentary, we might cite the following articles: U. Vanni, *Il 'Padre nostro'*, in 'La Civiltà cattolica' 3 (1993) 345-358 and 477-490; J. Castellano Cervera, *La preghiera del Signore: 'Padre nostro'*, in "L'Osservatore Romano" 3 Feb 1993.

11. A. Gentili – A. Schnöller, *Dio nel silenzio*, Milan 1993, pp. 197-201; A. Gentili, *Pregate così*, Bologna 1978, pp. 69-84.

12. M. Albertz cit. in C. Brütsch, *La clarté de l'Apocalypse*, Geneva 1966, p. 305.

13. *Lumen Gentium*, 53

14. John Paul II, *Mulieris Dignitatem*, 3: "The self-revelation of God, which is the inscrutable unity of the Trinity, is fundamentally contained in all its essentials, in the annunciation at Nazareth."

15. J. Gerson, *Tractatus super Magnificat*, Tract IX (Esurientes implevit bonis) in *Opera Omnia*, Antwerp 1706, IV, col. 418.

Part Two

THE OUR FATHER
AND ITS TWIN PERSPECTIVES

Exegetes are, quite rightly, concerned to establish the original context of Jesus' deeds and sayings. At the same time, we also know that the words and acts recorded in the Gospels are simply what has come down to us from the apostles' preaching to the first generation of Christians. The important thing is that these preoccupations do not either ignore the first witnesses' experience of Christ, nor ignore the emphases and nuances with which the message has passed into the lives of believers.

In the Gospels, we have two versions of the Our Father, that of Matthew and that of Luke. The structure of each is essentially the same, and both were given in the context of prayer. Matthew gives the Lord's prayer within the Sermon on the Mount, where he speaks about the validity of Christian prayer in contrast to that of pharisees and pagans (cf Mt 6:9-13), while Luke places it at the start of his catechesis on prayer itself (cf Lk 11:1ff). The text of Matthew is the one we normally recite.

OUR FATHER
THE PRAYER OF THE PASSION

If we ask ourselves about the "Christ" dimension of the Our Father and set out to seek for traces of it in our Lord's own prayer, in so far as the Gospels tell us about this, we find that the Our Father gains a particular relevance in the context of the passion. So much so, that we must conclude that this was when Christ's prayer flowed most freely and was most vibrant.[1] Therefore, this will be our best clue towards understanding the place of the Our Father in our Lord's own prayer.

Having said that, we must now show how this is so, and we will do so by looking at each invocation in turn. St Ignatius has already invited us to reflect on the words of the prayer "and continue meditating in this word as long as he finds various meanings, comparisons, relish and consolation in the consideration of it".[2]

1. *Our Father, in heaven*

All the evangelists tell us that in Gethsemane, Christ called upon Abba-Father: Mt 26:39; Mk 14:36 (the only one to give us the phrase "Abba-Father"); Lk 22:42; Jn 12:27.

This invocation "Father" occurs in two gospel texts before the passion: in Mt 11:25 "I bless you Father..." and in Jn 11:41 "Father, I thank you...". Nor must we forget that the word "Father" figured in the twelve-year-old Jesus' words in the Temple (Lk 2:49) and in his supreme invocation on the Cross (Lk 23:46).

2. *Hallowed be your name*

During his passion Christ prayed: "Father, glorify your Son" (Jn 17:1). In the last discourse before the passion, as given us by John, the word "glory" occurs no less than thirteen times.

There is a close relationship between the glorification of God and the sanctifying, or hallowing, of his name. A name expresses the person who bears it and Christ, recognising the holiness of the Father, fulfils the mission to which he has been called.

3. *Your kingdom come*

During the passion, it becomes quite clear that Christ had come to open the kingdom of heaven to us, that he places himself in opposition to the dominion of Satan (Jn 12:31; 16:11). The world is judged and Satan's dominion overthrown. To the penitent thief, Christ opens the gates of the kingdom (Lk 23:42).

4. *Your will be done on earth as it is in heaven*

The account of his prayer in Gethsemane shows clearly how this phrase, central to the Our Father, is the heart of Jesus' prayer. Christ begs the Father that whatever the cost the divine will be done, whether on earth or in heaven. It is only those who do the will of the Father who enter the kingdom of heaven (Mt 7:21).

5. *Give us this day our daily bread*

Daily has a richer meaning here, it means our essential bread, or the bread of tomorrow. As if we said: give us the bread of the kingdom which is to come, and in fact a great banquet is an image of the kingdom which is to come (Mt 22:1ff; Lk 16:16ff).

The bread of the future kingdom is the Eucharist, given to us at the Last Supper, itself celebrated within the context of the Passion.

6. *Forgive us our trespasses,*
   as we forgive those who trespass against us

There are many references to this petition scattered throughout the Gospels, in the discourses, the parables and the actions of Christ. There is a more direct reference to "the forgiveness of sins" in the consecration of the chalice at the Last Supper, and still more in Christ's prayer from the cross "Father, forgive them, for they know not what they do" (Lk 23:34).

Nor must we forget that one of the characteristics of the new covenant as it was presented by the prophets, is the forgiveness of sins.

7. *And lead us not into temptation,*
   but deliver us from the Evil One

At the beginning of his Passion, Christ put his disciples on guard against the danger of falling into temptation (Mt 26:31).

The scene in Gethsemane is presented as an "entering into temptation" (Mt 26:41; Mk 14:38; Lk 22:40). Only prayer can prevent us from succumbing to temptation (for the words should be translated "keep us from succumbing to temptation").

Temptation reminds us of the Tempter, who is not explicitly named in the scene at Gethsemane, but who is named here in this concluding phrase of the Our Father. We are reminded of the forty days spent by Christ in the desert, where he was subjected to "every temptation of

Satan" who then "left him for a while to return at his appointed time" (Lk 4:13), that is, the time of the Passion.

Exercise 5:
Relive the Passion

Looking at the Gospel texts, we can see the close link between the Our Father and the Passion of the Lord. In our meditation we will find our own echoes as we explore these connections.

1. *Our Father* ...
"Pray, saying: Abba, Father" (Mk 14:36,39).

2. *Hallowed* .. .
"Father, sanctify your Name!" (Jn 12:28).

3. *Come* ...
"You are a king ... remember me when you come into your kingdom" (Jn 18:33; Lk 23:42).

4. *Be it done* ...
"Father, let this cup pass from me! Nevertheless, not my will but yours be done" (Lk 22:42).

5. *Give us this day* ...
"Take and eat. This is my body which is given for you" (Mt 26:26; Lk 22:19).

6. *Forgive us* ...
"This is my blood of the new covenant, shed for many for the forgiveness of sins" (Mt 26:28). "Father, forgive them for they know not what they do" (Lk 23:34).

7. *And lead us not* ...
"Pray, lest you enter into temptation" (Lk 22:40). "The prince of this world has no power over me" (Jn 14:30).

OUR FATHER
AN ESCHATOLOGICAL PRAYER

If Christ is the context within which the full and profound meaning of the Our Father is best revealed to us, then this is particularly true of the Passion. So much so, that we may now ask about the original Christian meaning of this prayer? In other words, what thoughts and feelings did it evoke in the first generation of disciples of the Resurrection? Recent studies have highlighted the eschatological character of this prayer which Christ gave us. (Eschatology = the ultimate reality, something to be made known at the final coming of the kingdom of God.) In the Our Father, we find reflected the "eager longing" (Rom 8:19; Phil 1:20) for the second coming of Jesus Christ because, in the early years of Christian history, this was thought to be imminent.[3]

Many things support this reading, especially the verb tenses used in the original Greek text. In the petitions of the Our Father, the tense used is known as the "eschatologic-aorist". The aorist in Greek is a special tense which indicates that an action is completed once and for all, in a definitive way, rather like the perfect in Latin. It is a grammatical form uniting the present to eternity. In the Christian today – a "today" which we find in the Our Father in the invocation for bread – eternity is already present. Time, from within which those who believe in Christ scan eternity, is not an indifference, or a colourless succession of moments, or a cyclic recurrence of events. Rather, it could be called the ante-chamber of eternity; it is the seed of eternity. The eschatologic-aorist in the petitions of the Our Father was not meant to imply a gradual process of immersion in the divine mystery (although that is not excluded). Rather, it seeks to indicate the ultimate character of Christian experience and the way in which our perception of the today of God is our focus and supreme moment.

Let us now look at each invocation.

1. *Our Father in heaven*

At once the reference to God as a Father who is in heaven, immediately shifts us into the dwellings of eternity. It seems to suggests to us that God is no longer to be found on Sinai or, to recall Christ's life, in the time of Gethsemane, nor on the Mount Garizim (cf Jn 4:1-42, the episode with the Samaritan woman). The roads to heaven are re-opened with Christ. Communication with God is direct (in spirit), authentic (in truth) and effective. Further, to call on God as our Father means that we look towards our destiny as children of a perfect adoption. We are called as a people who will discover themselves through the bonds of communion which unite the family of God.

2. *Hallowed be your name*

The hallowing, making holy, of the divine name, the definitive recognition of God's transcendence and the definitive inauguration of God as Lord, is the fulfilment of everything. In seeking the hallowing of God's name and the spreading of God's attracting power throughout the world, the Christian acknowledges that God comes first in his or her own life. In the words of Clement: we pass "from ignorance to full knowledge of the glory of this name".[4] The Christian stands resolutely on God's side and God will bring his plans of grace to fulfilment in such a Christian. This applies to every petition of the Our Father.

3. *Your kingdom come*

This eschatological tension and the polarisation towards ultimate reality move the Christian community to identify itself with the kingdom of God, for God's kingdom is already present and at work within that community. While the Christian *eschaton* is indeed the fulfilment of the divine plan revealed to us in Christ, it is neither separate from the coming of the Word in the flesh, nor subsequent to that coming. Rather, that coming is the first coming and it coincides with the *eschaton* which unravels itself from our human time (the aorist!). Thus each "today" of ours has a flavour of eternity; within it, the divine stirs and shines through our human vicissitudes.[5]

4. *Your will be done,*
on earth as it is in heaven

The will of God floods human life, joining itself to us through irrevocable decisions. This petition of the Our Father goes far beyond any moralistic imperative or even any determination to do the will of God. It expresses the definitive inauguration of the heavenly order in earthly events. In the last analysis, what is the will of God but love?

"The structure of the Our Father is modelled on the twin commandments of love: 'Love the Lord your God with all your heart, with all your soul and with all your mind' Jesus replied to the doctors of the law. 'This is the first commandment. The second is equally important: love your neighbour as yourself. The whole law of Moses and all the teaching of the prophets depend on these two commandments' (cf Mt 22:34-40)."[6] So we can say that the Our Father is the twin commandment of love given as prayer.

To follow in the footprints of Christ is our supreme rule. For our salvation, he became obedient unto death, and to death on a cross (cf Phil 2:8). The daily cross accepted in love, our self-giving, our love poured out in total self-sacrifice, these are the will of God expressed concretely in a particular life. These are the yardstick of "final" judgement (cf Mt 25:31).

The first three petitions concern the eschatological glory of God. The remaining petitions shift the spotlight onto us.

5. *Give us this day our daily bread*

This today of which the Our Father speaks is time as the essential measure, separating us from eternity but already enclosed in the eschatological future. Today, we express our radical choice and receive a pledge of the life to come. Today, we ask for the bread of the kingdom, that mysterious bread, called *epioúsios* in the Greek phrase, which means that eschatological food with which we shall be gladdened in eternal life.[7]

Such food is the Eucharist under another name, a temporal and transient sign of the perfect and complete reality – the glorified body of Christ. This sign anticipates, even as it brings to realisation, the full self-communication of God to creation. The aorist of Mt 6:11 (Lk 11:3 has the present tense because he refers to the "bread of every day") reinforces this reading. It suggests that the Christian is not seeking an ephemeral food but knows instead that all our todays are a unique, unrepeatable and definitive opportunity to respond to the hunger of God. The joy of knowing that we are filled with heavenly food is the most comforting response to the condition of poverty, weakness and existential unease which marks our pilgrimage here on earth.

6. *And forgive us our trespasses,*
   as we forgive those who trespass against us

Unlike the first three invocations (name, kingdom, will) the last three, in the Greek text, have an "and" which holds them in tension. In particular, the "and" which links this one to the following reveals the complementary aspects of our rapport with God. If we are to be admitted to the heavenly banquet, our hearts need to be reconciled with God and our brother or sister. Nor should we forget that the second part of this invocation of the Our Father shows that we can open ourselves to prayerful rapport with God only after we have forgiven our sisters or brothers and have thereby come to a state of irrevocable reconciliation (cf Mk 11:25). Offences only become "trespasses" when we know we are united as children, brothers, sisters. The fatherhood of God and the brotherhood of man require the practice of forgiveness. They will be fully realized with the coming of the eschatological kingdom.

Here, too, the word, or better the words show how unique and definitive is the pardon thus received. Note, too, that this is the only petition of the Our Father to command us so directly and explicitly. These words also show the irrevocable character of the divine action, that this, as we have seen, is transmitted to us without recall.

This sixth petition of the Our Father shows an awareness that the divine judgement is near; it is imminent, and so the petition carries the request for total pardon. Through this saving judgement, our sins proclaim our total dependence on God's saving action. Only through this saving judgement, therefore, can we be truly forgiven – and this not only includes our moral faults, but everything which follows from our limitations as creatures.

7. And lead us not into temptation
but deliver us from the Evil One

This last invocation shows even more clearly that the whole meaning of the Christian life is conquest in the decisive, ultimate and definitive battle with the Evil One. This is the same as saying that we become free in this world from the dominion of Satan, its prince. To overcome the Evil One means to conquer that supreme obstacle separating the triumph of Christ from the beginning of God's kingdom.

The struggle with temptation means more than a flight from evil or the daily overcoming of things which lead us into sin. Rather it means that, with head held high, we approach our human life as the place within which the final, eschatological struggle between God and Satan is being fought out, the place where God is victorious over the other. This is why Scripture says: "When you face trials of any kind, consider it nothing but joy" (Jas 1:2). We find the same words on Christ's lips in Gethsemane. When we are in a similar difficult situation, then, the sacred author tells us: "the work of God reaches its perfection and we become perfected" (Jas 1:4). In Christian terminology, the words "perfection" and "perfected" suggest the eschatological thrust towards the supreme good.

So the last three petitions of the Our Father are focused around a single theme: the divine gift – bread, forgiveness, deliverance – has its destiny in the "we" of the eschatological community, where we are all children of the one Father.

NOTES TO PART TWO

1. H. Kruse, *"Pater noster" et Passio Christi*, in "Verbum Domini" 46 (1968) 3-29.
2. Ignatius of Loyola, *Spiritual Exercises*, trans. Louis J. Puhl SJ, Loyola University Press, Chicago 1951, n. 252.
3. R. E. Brown, *The Pater noster as an eschatological prayer*, in N.T. *Essays*, London-Dublin 1965, pp. 217-253.
4. Clement of Rome, *First letter to the Corinthians*, 59, 2.
5. In the biblical tradition, time is expressed in three ways: a return to the beginning (in principio); the "length of days" through which the story of humanity and creation develops, and the third, which is the point at which the two meet and which is, above all, that intended by the word "today". In this today, ordinary time is suspended and the now of divine experience flowers: the heavens are opened. It is in this "instant" that knowledge is opened up (by intuition, illumination, realisation, revelation) and the divine invades the human. Personal prayer "in

spirit and in truth", and still more, liturgical prayer, is the privileged place for such an experience. Cf G. Vannucci, *L'istante e l'anamnesis nell'esperienza religiosa*, in *La parola creatrice*, Cernusco sul Naviglio 1993, pp. 154-167.

6. B. Bartolini, *Guidare alla comprensione delle formule di preghiera, specialmente del 'Padre nostro'*, in "Dossier catechista" 6 (1992) 27. See also the previous three contributions, nn. 7 (pp. 27-31), 8 (pp. 27-30) and 9 (pp. 17-21). The author has developed a practical approach to reciting the Our Father with gestures in *Sono qui, Gesù*, supplement on prayer, in the catechism *Venite con me*.

7. "Daily" is the usual and traditional translation of the difficult term *epioúsios*, which probably means "necessary to existence". In the ancient church, it was often used to mean the bread of the Eucharist. St Jerome says that in the Aramaic Gospel of Nazareth we find the term *mahar* which means "tomorrow". So the meaning of this would be: "give us today the bread of tomorrow". "In the Hebrew Gospel according to Matthew, we read the same: 'Give us today our bread of tomorrow', that is, give us today that bread which you will give us in your kingdom", *Vangelo degli Ebrei e Nazarei*, 17, in *Apocrifi del Nuovo Testamento*, Turin 1971, pp. 378-379, where it cites Jerome, *Tract. in Ps. 135.*

Part Three

THE OUR FATHER
TEACHES US

The Our Father begins with the Father and ends with the Evil One. It is like a fan, covering the divine plan and human destiny in one superb, comprehensive span. We now want to highlight the teaching aspect of the Our Father and the way in which it consolidates our bond as children of the Father. We are bound to the Father for we have been made one with Christ who gave us a guide in the Spirit of love poured into our hearts.

In order to understand this triple dimension of Father-Christ-Spirit more clearly, it can help us if, in our personal prayer, we recite or meditate on the Our Father and only contemplate the Father. Let him be the one to whom our prayers are going. To make it even clearer, we can repeat the word "Father" before each invocation. At another time, we may choose simply to warm ourselves in the spirit of Christ and relive his deep feelings as if he, Christ, were praying in me and through me. "Reciting the Our Father, we must not forget to be close to the one who taught it to us" recommends St Teresa.[1] Here the Our Father is at its most sacramental. It is like the prayer of the heart which, through repetition of the holy name brings the person into the presence of Jesus.[2] This can be so to such an extent that at the end of the prayer I am thinking as Jesus, feeling as Jesus and, in consequence, acting as Jesus. Such a transformation is not the work of a moment. Also, it is costly. It demands an intense participation in the mystery of Christ, of which the Our Father is the quintessence, a condensed version.

On another occasion, we might refer to the Holy Spirit

who "groans within us: Abba-Father" (Rom 8:15; Gal 3:16). In a moment, we shall offer a short exercise on this. In order to deepen our focus on the Holy Spirit, we would stress that each recitation of the Our Father is a pentecostal event. This is partly because every word of Christ releases his Spirit; as he said: "he whom God has sent speaks the words of God, for he gives the Spirit without measure" (cf Jn 3:34; Jn 6:63). It is also because the Spirit is the Spirit of adoption which is poured out in abundance in order to bring about the messianic era.

Another way of approaching this, and one which would still partake of the intention to demonstrate the Trinitarian nature of Jesus' prayer, is to place into each invocation a direct reference to one of the divine persons, in this way:

Name – Father	Bread – Father
Kingdom – Son	Forgiveness – Son
Will – Spirit	Spirit of Evil – Spirit of God

Each pair can stand alone, and each has a sound biblical basis. Although that can, at this point, be left on one side, it would justify a meditation of its own.

Departing from this ever-expanding understanding of Jesus' prayer, let us now focus on one last aspect. The Our Father is the Christian prayer *par excellence*. Like Kierkegaard, we recognize that the person who truly prays is not the one who demands to be heard by God, but rather the one who wants to listen to God. This, therefore, is the prayer in which we say "yes" to the Father, like sons and daughters who know and understand. We say "yes" to God's thoughts and gifts. There is an ancient Spanish liturgy, still in use, which provides for a recitation of the Our Father with "Amen" interspersed at every invocation. "Our Father in heaven: R. Amen" and so on, an unusual insight of powerful effect. It can be used either privately or in community recitation, letting the "Amen" express our consent to all God asks of us and to all that is lavished upon us.

A MODEL FOR
THE PATH OF INITIATION

A great master of prayer, called Fr J. B. Lotz, speaks of praying the Our Father by beginning at the end and reversing the order of the invocations. We can recite them rhythmically on the movement of our breath, or just take a single word or a phrase "because each part of it resonates with the whole of it".[3] Perhaps this is how the Our Father reveals itself as a true model for initiating us into our journey. As we go in turn through each of its pedagogic doorways, we are led from darkness into the inaccessible light where God dwells. This journey is engraved in the heart of every religion. As Christians, we have an embarrassment of choices. It is enough to quote Peter: "God has called you out of darkness into his marvellous light" (1 Pet 2:9), or Paul: "I am sending you to the Gentiles... so that they may turn from darkness to light" (Acts 26:18). Let the summons of Hinduism speak for other religions: "Lead me out of darkness into the light; from death may I come to immortality" (*Bhradaranyaka Upanishad* 1,3,28).

In this case the Our Father starts with liberation from the Evil One and the consequent freedom from every temptation brought us by Christ who began his messianic vocation with forty days in the desert (Lk 4:13). This then leads us to the knowledge of our own unworthiness and the drastic purification of heart needed if we are to open ourselves more fully to grace. Let us take Angela of Foligno and her experience as a shining example of the revelatory character of this prayer of Jesus'. There is a moment when she speaks of receiving a "marvellous enlightenment" while reciting the Our Father. This is what she says: "One time I had gone to church and prayed God to grant me a grace of some kind. While I was praying the Our Father I received deep in my heart a very clear awareness of the divine goodness and my own unworthiness. I understood the meaning of each of the words I was saying deep in my heart. I recited the Our Father so slowly and consciously that even though on the one hand I wept bitterly because I was so aware of my sins and my unworthiness, still, on the other hand, I felt a great consolation and I began to taste something of the divine sweetness. I perceived the divine goodness in this prayer better than anywhere else, and I still perceive it better there even today. [...] At each of these previous steps, I lingered for a good while before I was able to move on to the next step. In some of the steps I lingered longer, and for a shorter time in others."[4]

After reading that wonderful page, it is quite clear that the measure of a liberated heart is its ability to live in peace and harmony with itself, with others, with creation and with God. Only from this position can we prepare ourselves to enter the family of God. "Blessed are the peacemakers, for they shall be called children of God" (Mt 5:9). The children of God have access to the table of the kingdom (cf Mt 15:26). They have entered the realm of the freely given, the realm of gift, consent, welcome.

The power of this bread, which is Christ himself, enables us to shift our centre of gravity from ourselves to God, so that we no longer seek things for ourselves but instead we offer ourselves, without conditions, to the designs of God. The source inspiring our thoughts and actions is no longer our limited and unreliable self, but the will of God, which is the will of Love. This brings about total dedication to the cause of the Kingdom, into which we pour our best energies of mind and heart, all now strengthened by grace. Thus the divine design draws everything to a focus, leads all things to their fullest realization. The universal fatherhood of God draws everything to itself. God is now "all in all" (1 Cor 15:28) and each creature now lives in the bosom of the Father (Jn 1:18).

The seven sacraments

Always moving from the basis described above, the invocations of the Our Father can help us trace the experience of initiation which is summed up in the seven sacraments. The reference to the Evil One reminds us of *baptism* in which we are set free from slavery to Satan and gathered to the Spirit of the Resurrection. Throughout our lives, which are always threatened by sin, baptism is brought to us again by the sacrament of *penance*, alluded to in the phrase "deliver us from evil...". The gift of new life continually offered the believer, is the ability to share at the table of the Lord and to be nourished on our "daily bread" in the *Eucharist*.

Moving to the next invocation, the prayer that the will of God be done is linked to the outpouring of the Holy Spirit. By this outpouring, the new law is written in our hearts which comes to fruition in *confirmation*. This is the sacrament which strengthens, or confirms, us in our determination to cling lovingly to the designs of God. The invocation about the kingdom and the coming of the kingdom relate to the two sacraments which focus on the building of that kingdom: *marriage* and *ordination*. The final petition is about the name of God, destined to shine on the foreheads of the elect. Here our thoughts turn to the *anointing of the infirm and the elderly* who are coming to the end of their earthly lives and approaching the crowning of their faith.

In community recitation, the one who is guiding the prayer could say each invocation (starting it with the word "Father"), while those present respond from time to time with *Amen*, said as a renewal of their "yes" to the grace of each sacrament. For the last invocation, one might close the meditation by saying: "Therefore you are our heavenly Father, who lives and reigns for ever and ever."

Exercise 6:
Speaking the Our Father rhythmically on a breath

Although breathing is not praying, prayer will never become the breath of our existence without the complete integration of all our component parts, physical, psychological and spiritual. As the Abbot Anthony used to say: "Always breathe Jesus Christ and believe in him".

We are familiar with the teaching of Scripture, which speaks of our breath of life as the breath of God, the original sacrament of God's Spirit poured out on us at birth. This is still more so of the sacramental outpouring of the Spirit at Pentecost, that incessant breathing of the risen Christ on his disciples (Gn 2:7; Jn 20:22). So we can even speak of a breath of communication between us and God, at least in the sense that "the breath of life comes to us from God" (cf Acts 17:25). Job understood this well when he said: "The breath of the Omnipotent brought me into life" (33:4) and the continual ebb and flow of "the breath of God in my nostrils" (27:3) maintains me in existence. But the breath of communication with God also means that this breath leads us to God. This is what the pious Israelite meant when he said: "With open mouth I pant, because I long for your commands" (Ps 119:131). If this is so for the devout Israelite, how much more can it apply to the Christian who, as we have seen, lives under the direct breathing of the Holy Spirit?[5] The Spirit is poured out on us at baptism and confirmation, and constantly renewed through our sacramental life. It is like water, always rising up fresh and sparkling from the one source.

For this reason, the two phases of breathing are both important, they are subtle and symbolic. Breathing in and breathing out are like two moments in a single movement. They are like two ways of running the path of interior prayer in the presence of God.

After this introduction, let us look again at the experience of speaking, but in spiritual terms. Of its nature, speaking implies that the lungs are filled with air, and that this same air then emerges modulated as the words we want to pronounce. In our case, the air we breathe in is seen as the outpouring of the Holy Spirit on us. When we breathe out, the Spirit groans within us, saying: "Abba-Father" (Rom 8:15).

In practice, we proceed in this way: "We breathe in the Holy Spirit (cf Ps 119:131) and allow the first invocation "Our Father, in heaven" to resonate as the breath of the Spirit within us. When we have said the words, we remain, listening to the inner echo. We do this slowly, calmly, not in any forced way, always under the breath of the Spirit, but quite naturally. When the lungs are empty, our prayer focuses in a pause of silent adoration. This is the pause of repose, of completion, of personal assimilation, awaiting another inspiration. The word vibrate, resonate, quiver, is an exact one. This breathing is so done that the breath itself becomes our own language, growing out of a new self-awareness. It is a language deeply rooted in our very being.

NOTES TO PART THREE

1. Teresa of Jesus, *The Way of Perfection*, 34, 10
2. Cf Anonimo, *Lo Joga cristiano. La preghiera esicasta*, ed. G. Vannucci, Florence 1978, pp. 54-58.
3. J. B. Lotz, *Guida alla meditazione*, Milan 1968, p. 182.
4. Angela of Foligno, Classics of Western Spirituality, Paulist, New York 1993, pp. 127-8.
5. St Thomas says that the new law is itself the grace of the Holy Spirit (*Summa Theologica* I-II, 106, 1: "Lex nova principaliter ipsa gratia est Spiritus sancti").

Part Four

THE OUR FATHER
IN GESTURE

In the perspective of the Hebreo-Christian religion we, men and women, hold a place of privilege in God's sight. "And God said, 'Let us make humankind in our image, according to our likeness' [...] so God created humankind in his image, in the image of God he created them; male and female he created them" (Gen 1:26ff). And God, continues the priestly version of the Genesis account, "saw everything that he had made and indeed it was very good" (Gen 1:31). Being in the image of God means that we are to operate in the world as a kind of representative of God, so that those we meet can say that they have also met God. So in our love for others, we also love God, we serve God in our service of others.

With the incarnation of the Son of God, humanity was "absorbed" into the heavenly sphere. At the same time, we were restored to our ancient dignity and re-united with our most profound identity as human-divine. Truly, we can cry out, wonder-stricken, that it is we, fully alive, who are the glory of God. This is not an unjustified claim. Rather, according to the apostle Paul, it is because "all of us, with unveiled faces, seeing the glory of God reflected as in a mirror, are being transformed into the same image from one degree of glory to another" (2 Cor 3:18).

We who are the "image and likeness" of God, have been given a body which is the synthesis and self-aware summit of creation.[1] Our body is "the centre from which the divine energy radiates throughout the universe",[2] the locus of the cosmic "priesthood".

These introductory remarks enable us to understand more clearly the importance which we shall give to saying the Lord's prayer with gestures. In much human communication we accompany our words with gestures and do so instinctively. It is a way of involving ourselves more, of being more intimately associated with our own words. We reveal ourselves in our gestures, "speaking" long before we express ourselves in words. Sometimes the gestures which accompany our words form a wonderful unity with them, a complete communication. For this reason, gesture is the inheritance of every culture. Great importance is attached to it, that it be relevant and aware. It is a natural instrument, instinctive to us, but it needs to be educated if it is to attain its full potential.[3]

A peaceful gesture, repeated with awareness in the context of prayer, helps to calm the mind, enabling a deeper awareness and intuition to emerge. The whole person is then in harmony, resonating with the content of the message. In this way we come to a communication which is living, not merely conceptual, and this applies equally to our communication with God. Even more does it apply to that prayer *par excellence* by which redeemed men and women, sons and daughters in the Son,[4] interact with their Father who is in heaven. There are many and varied ways in which we can add gestures to the Our Father, but here we offer three.

Exercise 7:
The position of the one who prays

The most simple gesture is one familiar from the celebration of the Eucharist. In the *Principles and Norms for using the Roman Missal 1983*, the CEI has established that: "during the singing or recitation of the Our Father, the arms may be extended. This gesture is appropriate if made in a climate of community prayer, provided there be an opportunity to explain it".[5] These norms are like the basic principles which offer support and guidance to the various applications.

"To stand upright with the arms open, hands extended and eyes raised up, is a way of praying both among the Jews or among people of past ages, such as Rome or, later, the Christians. This position reveals the relationship between God and the one who prays. Anthropologically speaking, it is certainly important for us all. It is clear from the early texts, however, that Christians regarded this attitude in prayer as particularly their own, because it recalled Jesus Christ praying with his arms extended on the cross. They therefore deliberately adopted this same bodily attitude for their own prayers, eager in this way to conform more closely to Christ, the one who prayed perfectly. Just because he had used it, he had filled any similar gesture with his own 'Christic' meaning".[6]

We would only add a word about standing up. This is how we pray the Our Father in the liturgy and it is a natural position to adopt in our private prayer, as well. Standing upright is the spontaneous human position; it is the way children stand before their Father, but above all it is the position of the Risen Lord. We listen to the Gospel standing up, and much of our public prayer finds us standing and thereby expressing a corresponding inner attitude.

Exercise 8:
Expressing the depths

A more elaborate choreography of gestures with four movements can be seen in the diagram. The first three invocations: *Our Father...*; *Hallowed...*; *Your kingdom...*; all suggest that the arms should be lifted up in the classic position of prayer (as in fig. 1).

With the central invocation: *Your will...* we place our arms in the form of a cross and recall that culminating expression of the divine will, as we see it in Christ at the time of his death (fig. 2).

We do not stay in this position, however, but allow it to lead us on to the appropriate attitude for the next invoca-

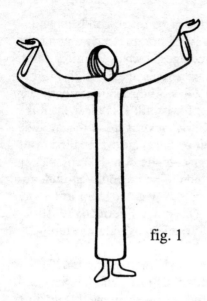

fig. 1

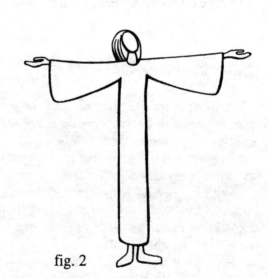

fig. 2

tions: *Give us this day...*; and *forgive us...* Now we hold our arms in front of us, like one gathering "supersubstantial bread", and still more like one gathering forgiveness – which we will then offer to others (fig. 3).

Next, at: *Lead us not... but deliver us...* we lower our arms towards the ground, expressing the abandonment of faith (fig. 4).

fig. 3

fig. 4

Keeping in mind this first introduction to gesture, let us recall what was said in a previous chapter about the *traditio* of the Our Father during the Eucharistic celebration. Let us also remember how we underlined the congregation's Amen, at each invocation. If we do this, we have quite enough tools for praying the Our Father in whatever position or place seems most appropriate.

A recitation which has a different gesture for each invocation is a little more complex. Here is an example:

1. *Our Father in heaven*: the classic position of prayer, with arms raised and elbows lightly flexed.

2. *Hallowed be your name*: hands joined beneath the chin and head bowed.

3. *Your kingdom come*: extend the arms in the form of a cross and gaze upwards.

4. *Your will be done on earth as it is in heaven*: cross the arms in front of the chest, look up (to heaven) and then bow the head (to earth).

5. *Give us this day our daily bread*: hands cupped in front of the chest.

6. *Forgive us our trespasses, as we forgive those who trespass against us*: strike the breast with the right hand and let the left hand hang down beside the body. The head is bowed.

7. *And lead us not into temptation, but deliver us from evil*: at first the arms lie along the body, in the attitude of one who is disarmed and powerless, then raise them lightly with the hands in an attitude of keeping something off, as if fending off an approaching danger.

8. *For yours is the kingdom, the power and the glory*: lift the arms in the form of a V-shape, and turn towards the heavens.[7]

*Our Father
in heaven*

*Hallowed
be your name*

*Your
kingdom
come*

*Your will
be done on earth
as it is in heaven*

*Give us
this day
our daily bread*

*Forgive us
our trespasses*

*As we forgive
those who trespass
against us*

*And lead us
not into
temptation*

*But deliver us
from evil*

*For yours is
the kingdom,
the power
and the glory*

Exercise 9:
The Our Father for inner healing

Kenneth McAll was born in China in 1910, qualified in Edinburgh as a doctor and returned to China as a missionary. He, with his wife and son, was imprisoned by the Japanese for four years during the Second World War. After he had returned home, he qualified as a psychiatrist and has done much to deepen our understanding of the experience of spiritual healing. He suggests that we pray as shown in the little sketches.

As these sketches are copied, we need to guess a little as we begin to use them, but the pale lines indicate a resting position and the dark lines show the movement. The drawings clearly show the dynamic by which prayer leads us to the Lord. Some gestures particularly will have a special power. Next to each sketch is the appropriate invocation.

1. We are aware of God the Father who raises us up;

2. respect for the holy name of God;

3. the heavenly kingdom of which, even here on earth, we have been made a member;

4. as (hands raised) the divine will is fulfilled in heaven, so it is a sweet yoke on my shoulders, too;

5. as we have said, this bread is to me like life, salvation, healing;

6. our sins are engraved on our hearts;

7. with a blow, we strike ourselves on the solar plexus, where our life is in touch with preceding generations and, therefore, with the sin which we have inevitably inherited from them;

8. an attitude of supplication, disarmed and powerless, one of trusting abandonment;

9. our finger, pointing to the ground, says: let the Evil One return to hell and no longer have any place in our lives;

10. the one praying is perfectly reconciled with God, with others, with the cosmos, and gathers everything into an wide gesture of love.

If we allow these to echo and make deep soundings within us, then little by little we will be healed from any evil which afflicts us, or which is locked up within us, and from any negative situation, past or present.[8]

EXCURSUS:
OUR BODIES*

Inner healing is sometimes called the healing of memories. St Augustine speaks about a similar experience, which we might say concerned the soul and all its baggage in terms of knowledge and the accumulated choices of a lifetime. "No-one would remember if he did not exist and were not alive."[9] To heal our memories means to refresh and cleanse our being from the roots, for we are partly made up of the events through which we have passed, the interactions we have had, interiorly and externally, with family and with those around us, both the natural and the supernatural.

The healing of memories leads us to consider, however briefly, a level of ourselves which is usually rather hidden and subtle. We wish to try and bring some clarity into an area which, in many ways, remains unexplored in ordinary catechesis.

Between an "earthly" and a "heavenly" body

It is important to state, right at the start, that the creation of our bodies and the creation of its informing principle,

---

* Before embarking on this fascinating and, in many respects unpublished, chapter on the roots of prayer in our body, we need to be more precise about the body to which we refer. We do not mean the body in any coarse sense, nor as purely material, but in its more subtle aspects. On this question, see the condensed, but illuminating, work of S. Spinsanti, *Il corpo come spirito*, in VV. AA., *Spiritualità. Fisionomia e compiti*, Rome 1981, esp.: "L'uomo e i suoi corpi: la conoscenza esoterica", pp. 206-208.

our human spirit, were simultaneous. At the same time, we profess our faith in the resurrection of the body, in which the "heavenly" body – which will make us a new creation, appearing "like the angels" (Mt 22:30) – will retain an identity which is substantially that of the "earthly" body. The continuity between these two, high-lighted by the resurrection, is rooted in that dimension of the human person which we call the psyche. It is in this sphere that, under the influence of divine grace, the spiritual body of the resurrection germinates, helped by our human co-operation. This spiritual body is the very body of Christ, victorious over death. St Paul speaks of it in these terms: "what is sown is perishable, what is raised is imperishable. [...] It is sown a physical body, it is raised a spiritual body" (1 Cor 15:42-44). Obviously he means that the psyche, or the "psychic body", is like a point of reference for the transforming work of grace. The psyche is the mark of continuity, of the individuality of the person.[10]

The body in which we root our prayer

In order to clarify the spirit-body link, and to draw out the importance of rooting our prayer in the deepest dynamic of the human person, we need to refer again to a triple structure of anthropology. This sees the human being as composed of body, psyche (soul) and spirit. These categories were familiar to classical thought and are, incidentally, taken from St Paul in a text which we read each Thursday evening at Compline (1 Thess 5:23). This was an insight which greatly interested the Fathers of the Church and gave rise to much reflection.[11]

In the light of their diagnosis, which is rich in wisdom for us, we can see that the physical body is like a shell, or the wrapping, of other, more subtle, "bodies".[12] We speak of a "physic" or "mental" body, thereby recalling the categories *psyké*/soul and *noús*/mind. These in turn can be seen as a kind of luminous[13] and non-physical shell, co-

70

extensive with the material body of which they are the form or pattern.

This was how St Augustine had spoken of it, after he had realized, "with certainty" that the soul is not material. The oneiric, or out-of-the-body, experience teaches us that the soul has "more the likeness of a body" – a likeness, note – "although it is not corporeal, but is something similar to a body".[14]

We might ask here how there can possibly be a body which is intermediate between the spiritual soul and the physical body? For a physicist or someone with a mechanist vision of human beings this would be quite inadmissible. However, the possibility of influence, and even of contact, is widely accepted, even without the direct mediation of a physical body. This is supported by the large body of documentation about paranormal and supernatural gifts.[15] To confine ourselves to our own sphere of interest, it is often said that the spiritual world works closely with the one who is conscious of it and in rapport with it, even if this is not close. In the same way, prayer brings good to each of the three dimensions of the human creature and, beginning with the spiritual, irradiates both the psyche and the body.

The human being is a network of relationships, at work openly and as hidden energy, the effects of which are felt both interiorly and exteriorly, consciously and unconsciously, unmistakably and subtly. This is borne out by depth psychology and the researches of modern physics.[16]

Entering the inner sanctuary

In the light of these entirely traditional considerations, incomplete but no less genuine for that, we are better placed to give a more penetrating evaluation of the inner experience.

The exercise which we shall offer takes note of the physical dimension while focusing on the spiritual. It offers a bridge from what we might call the cruder sphere to

71

the more subtle parts of our being. The Pseudo-Macarios writes: "The heart directs and governs all the organs of the body. If grace has entered the pastures of the heart, it will rule over all the members (of the body) and all the thoughts".[17] This means that our interior prayer is mediated to our physical selves while awakening and energising the psyche. It is rooted in that subtle body which forms the link between the material body and the spiritual one. This subtle body has a definite influence on all human behaviour and it is this body which will come into play at the resurrection of our mortal bodies.

The fullness and the attraction of this approach to spiritual exercises must be obvious to all. A master in this discipline had the same intuition when he detailed: "In all the Spiritual Exercises [...] we make use of acts of the intellect in reasoning and of the acts of the will in manifesting our love".[18] Heir to an uninterrupted and universal teaching, Ignatius of Loyola knew that "it is not much knowledge which fills and satisfies the soul, but the intimate understanding and relish of the truth",[19] and he gives us three ways of reaching our feelings and transforming them:

- solitude and silence;
- the examen of conscience, as an exercise in introspection and self-awareness;
- the application of the senses to penetrating the mysteries, the deeds and the words of the life of Jesus.

With regard to the first, we must set aside a time each day, not enduring the time but redeeming it. We devote this time to hearing both ourselves and God.

The second is a process of awareness, of recognizing ripples from the day's events so as to form an objective judgement about them, but always in a climate of prayer and freedom which comes to its conclusion in a sacramental confession.

With regard to the third, St Ignatius is speaking about

the different ways of praying which include the memory, understanding and will as well as the five bodily senses. Mobilising these last has the effect of leading us into a new inner sensitivity which shares in that of Christ (cf Phil 2:5) and of Mary.[20]

After this long digression, it will be easier to understand how the Lord's prayer, said and experienced with intensity and awareness, sheds divine light on our inner depths and purifies every level of our personality. We apply the spiritual principle within us through the invocations: *Father – name – kingdom – will*; the psyche-mental dimension through: *Forgive us – as we forgive*; and finally the physical-material with: *Bread – deliver us from evil/the Evil One*.

As a conclusion to this *Excursus*, we would like to quote Vannucci: "In human religious experience, the body is a metaphor, a symbol. It is something concrete but always open to the divine infinity and destined for the total transfiguration of the flesh. [...] This is why it is essential to know the body, both in its biological structure and in those dimensions which are beyond the senses, essential to know its potential for spiritual realisation. In such a perspective, the body will lead us upward, for it is a most marvellous instrument of our ascent. At the same time, it contains a multitude of signs which set out a programme for us to bring into fulfilment. The body, being both language, primary matter and instrument, is essentially human. Each one of us is at once our body, our soul and our spirit. The body and the psyche relate to a third dimension in which the body is the third element of the triad: spirit, soul and body. All are called to live in harmony. Only this can transmit and reveal the world of the divine."[21]

In order to apply these reflections about integrating the Our Father into our experience (and therefore into the concrete and global reality of human life), we can now consider this prayer in a way which might be called psycho-somatic.

NOTES TO PART FOUR

1. Cf *Gaudium et spes*, 14.
2. G. Vannucci, *Il corpo simbolo dell'invisibile*, in *La parola creatrice*, Cernusco sul Naviglio 1993, p. 135.
3. Cf B. Bartolini, *Educare al valore dei gesti nella preghiera*, in "Catechista" 5 (1992) 21-24
4. Cf *Gaudium et spes*, 22/1390.
5. *Principles and Norms*, n.1. (Italian Bishops' Conference explanatory note.)
6. J. Janssen, *Interiorità ed espressione corporea nella preghiera contemplativa*, in "L'Osservatore Romano", 20 January 1990.
7. A. Gentili – A. Schnöller, *Dio nel silenzio*, Milan 1993, pp. 200-201.
8. K. McAll, *Healing the Family Tree*, op. cit.
9. Augustine, *De Trinitate*, 10, 10, 13: PL 11, 981.
10. For completeness, we must add that the physical body, moulded by God and destined to incorruptibility, experiences the consequences of sin and is, therefore, subject to death. On the other hand, with the resurrection of the body, it is revealed not simply as something by which we must not be "hijacked" but as something to be reformed into a glorious body (cf 2 Cor 5:2-5; 1 Cor 15:53) the very body of Christ. The *Jerusalem Bible* notes that those whom the Lord, on his return, finds alive in faith, will be "reclothed" if one may so put it, in a spiritual body, over the body of the psyche. The latter will be absorbed into the former (cf 2 Cor 5:3). We see this when we reflect on the physical body which is our flesh and blood, the sheer "materialness" of the human being, through which we often experience our thrust towards sin and our pitiless drive towards death. This cannot inherit the kingdom of God (1 Cor 15:50). So it follows that the risen body will not be a "carnal" one but a spiritual one, a body in which the physical and the psychological are pervaded definitively by the Holy Spirit.
11. Cf H. de Lubac, *Antropologia tripartita*, in *Mistica e mistero cristiano*, Milan 1979, pp. 59-117. The text of Paul says: "May the God of peace himself sanctify you entirely; and may your *spirit, soul* and *body* be kept sound and blameless at the coming of our Lord Jesus Christ. He who has called you is faithful and he will do this" (1 Thess 5:23-24).
12. There is an allusion to a plurality of "bodies" or to the constitutive parts of a person, in the first pages of Genesis (2:7). This is also found in much spiritual teaching in the major religious traditions. As a result, the person is seen as having four stages. The lowest is the physical body (*adama*/terra). Next comes the vital principle of lower life (*nefesh*) and then that of the higher or rational (*ruah*). Finally comes the radiance of the divine within us (*neshama*). "Reflecting on these stages in the spirit of a man" said Rabbi Shimeon, "is to discover the mystery of eternal wisdom, which has formed us in the image of the supreme mystery."
13. Origen called it "sparkling": cf H. Crouzel, *Origene*, Rome 1985, p. 134. See the entire chapter "L'antropologia spirituale" pp. 129-144, and still more pp. 324-333. On the same matter, cf T. Spidlik – I. Gargano, *La spiritualità dei Padri greci e orientali*, Rome 1983, pp. 73-77.

In the Alexandrian spiritual tradition, there is a significant text of Rufinus, written as a classical treatise on the death and resurrection of the body as paralleled by the annual death (in winter) and resurrection (in spring) of a seed, sown in the earth. He "takes from Origen the concept of a formal principle, of the material character which subsists unchanged throughout all the changes to which the human body is subject by time (and other things). This assures the unity of the body through any transformation between babyhood and old age. This formal principle endures beyond the death of the body and ensures the resurrection of that same body at the end of the world. [...] So the body, which during this life is dense and heavy becomes, at the moment of the resurrection, a body of light, the spiritual body of which St Paul speaks. It is transformed in order to rejoice in the blessed vision of God. In the light of this, the body is obviously immortal and incorruptible" (Rufinus, *Spiegazione del credo*, Rome 1983, pp. 108-113). John Chrysostom, in his commentary on the 1 Corinthians 15:44, gave the same exposition. It would not be out of place to note, too, that the traditions of Asia speak of our having a material body as well as one more subtle, or intellectual. There is particular awareness of such a body in, for example, the so-called "intermediate state" of physical death. In fact, when the principle of life goes out of its corporeal shell, it is no longer imprisoned by the crudely material but supported by an immaterial body made up of material in an elemental state, imponderable and not perceptible by our senses. Cf *The Tibetan Book of the Dead*, 1,1.

14. *De Genesi ad litteram*, 12, 33, 62: PL 34, 481.
15. One thinks of the risen Christ, who came in and out through closed doors and ate in front of others, or of saints who bilocated, working in the place to which they had transferred, and even being given objects which they were later found to have still with them.
16. F. Capra, *The Tao of Physics*, London 1991. In the psychological arena, one would doubtless consult C.G. Jung, *Psychology and Religion*.
17. *Spiritual homilies*, 15, 20: PG 34, 589.
18. Ignatius of Loyola, *Spiritual Exercises*, op. cit., n. 3.
19. *Ibid*. n. 2.
20. Cf *Spiritual Exercises* n. 50 on the application of the memory (recalling the facts), the understanding (reflecting on them) and the will (our interior response). The classical text for the application of the senses is the meditation on hell in the *Spiritual Exercises*, nn. 66-70. St Ignatius also speaks about "the five senses of the imagination" which are indispensible for contemplating the mysteries of Christ, nn. 121-125.
21. G. Vannucci, *La parola creatrice*, Cernusco sul Naviglio 1993, pp. 142-143.

Part Five

THE OUR FATHER
CONSIDERED
PSYCHO-SOMATICALLY

THE INVISIBLE
BOUND INTO THE VISIBLE

Spiritual exercises are, as we have been considering, intimately bound into "mystical physiology". Let us now show how it may be done.

In the west, "a small sign of the cross is made by priest and faithful at the beginning of the Gospel reading" when "the thumb of the right hand traces a cross in the centre of the forehead, on the lips and on the breast". "The small sign of the cross sums up these three subtle aspects, that in proclaiming the word, the intelligence, the utterance and the love must be in perfect harmony. In the rite of baptism, the priest traces the cross on the forehead and near the heart of the one to be baptized. Then he lays his hands on his or her head and at the end of the rite, traces a cross with chrism on the top of the head. In confirmation, the bishop makes the sign of the cross on the forehead of the one being confirmed. In priestly ordination, it is made on the palms of the ordinands' hands." Finally, when the sick are anointed, they are asked for the last time to open themselves to the fullness of life and be healed of those wounds of sin which express themselves in sickness and death.

In eastern Christianity "the hesychast tradition stresses two subtle centres, and awareness of them must be sustained during the exercise of breathing". These are the heart and the navel, the centre of the vital organs. If we look to the Far East, there we find a spiritual tradition of extraordinary profundity, which "enumerates seven subtle centres, starting at the base of the spine and ending on the top of the cranium. Oriental tradition rests on this presupposition, based on experience: that we normally use only a limited part of our brains, and therefore possess immense faculties which are latent and unused. Through exercises of mental concentration, together with muscle exercises, various bodily positions and breath control, we can slowly come to an illumination of these dormant areas. Each of them, once brought into play, opens a new universe to us."

"These subtle centres are, in fact, in the brain although we perceive them as located in various regions of the body. Thus, for instance, when we hurt our ankle, we know that the true perception of pain is in the brain, in such a way that we experience the pain in that part of the nervous system connected to it, even though the pain is, in fact, in the brain itself. In practice, the concentration exercised on the centre is felt as though it were really in the base of the spine, the solar plexus, the heart, the throat/lips, the forehead and the top of the head."

The Christian tradition

There is a question which now suggests itself to us: why are these centres only partially known and used within Christianity? "How has it happened that there is no hint of them in ascetic or mystical theology?" On the other hand, we cannot think that the ritual gestures so familiar to Christian tradition have arisen purely by chance. They too are rooted in awareness and motivation. The way in which they parallel the placing of the higher subtle centres in the oriental tradition, must make us think seriously about an awareness which western rationalism has since obliterated. Western medicine knows that there is a rapport between specific dysfunctional physical conditions and the psyche of the sick person. We speak of the mentality of someone with tuberculosis or with a heart condition, a gastric ulcer and so on. The psychological is linked to the physical, the invisible to the visible. There is no room to disbelieve a statement which stresses the close link between the psyche and the endocrine glands, or the possibility of a deliberate re-awakening and harmonising of the two.

With this possibility in mind, and still more with the speculation that we ourselves might be able to experience these subtle centres and their energy, some words of Christ now acquire a more precise and a far wider significance. Consider the parable of the eye as the lamp of the body (Lk 11:36), is it not indicative that the spiritual eye is situated in the centre of the forehead? Consider the many parables about the heart, that the vision of God is given to the one whose heart is untouched by evil (Mt 5:8); the tongue reveals the dominant power in the heart (Mt 12:34); the heart goes after our dominant desires (Mt 6:21); God must be loved with all our heart (Mt 22:37); Christ said of himself that he was meek and humble of heart (Mt 11:29). All these indicate awareness of the heart-centre.

"Traditional Christian prayer only knows the higher subtle centres and the heart-affective one. The question arises: why does Christian ritual not protect those subtle centres sited below the diaphragm. The more so as it is from here that energies arise which can overturn the dominion of the higher centres, not least those nourishing vital energies of love and peace? The only exception to this is the prayer of ecstasy, the prayer of *hesychia* or the contemplative quiet of one enslaved by love. Those who practice this prayer are also those who have tapped the energy of the inner centres below the diaphragm. Perhaps it is because the religion of love has understood that in order to awaken the heart, it has no need to travel through the first three subtle centres, that transfiguration can be attained starting with the heart." Perhaps, concludes Vannucci, whom we have quoted extensively[1] "there are two paths destined for two different categories of souls. One the sublimation of energies hidden in the inferior centres (inferior not in importance but in location), and the other beginning in the region of the heart for exceptional souls who, by a gift of grace, have no fascination with the material". For these others, simply to activate the heart during the practice of interior prayer, will unify and balance all the other centres.

Two directions of development

Rather than speak about two categories of souls, we would prefer to speak of *two directions of spiritual development*. One from below upwards, and the other from above, downwards, although in practice these two directions meet and intersect each other. From below upwards, means that the earthy person can reach towards heaven, purifying and lifting up all that energetic potential which sustains them. From above downwards, means that we can be reborn by a gift of grace and this grace will permeate every dimension of our being. It is easy to see, in these two directions, the characteristics of two religious universes, that of the west which appeals to Grace, and that of the east which appeals to Nature. It is even easier to see the importance of bringing western Christianity together with the hesychast tradition which opens the way to the inferior centres.[2]

To anticipate something we shall presently develop further, we would mention here that saving Grace is presented to us in the Gospels with surprising realism. It initiates a process of regeneration that finds its focus in what we might call "the womb of life". What other meaning than salvation can we give to the *immaculate conception* (meaning that Mary is freed from every invasion of original sin)? This is disclosed through her *virginal fruitfulness*, brought about by the power of the Spirit of God who sowed in her the seed of the Father's Word. Her fruitfulness came to its culmination in a *holy birth*, as is explicitly affirmed in Luke 1:35: "Therefore the child to be born will be holy; he will be called the Son of God".[3] Nor should it surprise us that *the way of natural birth is made the way of rebirth*. As Tertullian said: "the flesh is the pivot of salvation".[4]

AWARENESS
MEANS EFFECTIVENESS

After drawing together these essential points, let us see how the prayer which Jesus taught us can be "somatized", that is, given a bodily relevance. What we are about to develop is, beyond doubt, already part of our experience, albeit implicit. Possibly we have sometimes felt intense and deep vibrations which spread through our entire organism in a way that we are hardly aware of. Practice comes before theory, but theory can re-awaken, illumine and give life back to our practice. In other words, the vital centres exist and are at work even though we are not fully aware of it. To be aware, however, means a greater richness because certain processes, both spiritual and physical, are more effective when we are more aware of them. Let us, then, offer a certain perspective on the experience of our vital centres and their corresponding spirituality. In this way we may be able to make them seem less unfamiliar.[5]

1st centre: *the top of the head*:
This anatomical position indicates spiritual maturity, rather as the eyes of faith see saints crowned by an aureole. This is the place *par excellence* for communication with the divine, and is familiar to all the mystics.

2nd centre: *forehead*:
The co-ordinator of the functions of mind, will and the psychic function; this is the where thoughts are generated.

3rd centre: *lips/throat*:
The words generated in the mind emerge as sounds and can be expressed by appropriate vibrations.

4th centre: *heart*:

This zone presides over our self-giving love, our feelings and our devotion.

5th centre: *solar plexus*:

Centre of emotions, the point where cosmic energies flow together; it is, so to speak, the reservoir of these energies.

6th centre: *sacral, the bowels*:

Seat of physical vitality, of the generative powers and of deep feelings.

7th centre: *root, womb of life*:

The point where the person is rooted, here the spinal column relates to the lymph system and is the fount of beneficent energies destined to flow throughout the whole organism.

The secret of this kind of prayer lies in establishing an immediate rapport between the petitions of the Our Father and the centre which is to be activated through our attention and emotional resonance. By means of such an, almost instinctual, gathering of ourselves, we are more alert when we hear or say some expression particularly full of meaning for us. It may be either insult or compliment, but our whole person vibrates to it. We see nothing to hinder or discourage us, and this is borne out (it bears another repetition) by the psalms which invite us to reveal to God the "tremblings of our hearts" through the words of our lips.

After having placed ourselves in the presence of the Father and made our own the sentiments of Christ, we leave the door open for the outpouring of the Spirit. This pervades our being through our breathing. We give all our attention to the words we are saying, uttering them with simplicity and in perfect harmony with their various messages.

Exercise 10:
The Our Father and the vital centres

1. *Our Father in heaven (top of the head)*

I focus my attention on this physical point. I visualize the divine presence as a flower with a thousand petals which appears above my head. I open myself to the out-pouring of the Spirit of adoption, through which I turn back to God, calling on God as my Father.

2. *Father, hallowed be your name (forehead)*

I focus my attention between my eyebrows, where sits the inner eye. My gaze opens inwards on the vision of God so that the divine holiness, the Name of God carved in my brow (Apoc 14:1; 22:4), shines on my face and makes me radiant and peaceful.

3. *Father, your kingdom come (lips/throat)*

My attention converges on the organs of speech, where the divine Word takes form and sound, prior to being announced.

4. *Father, your will be done on earth as it is in heaven (heart)*

We have arrived at the heart where the two dimensions of our lives meet: the horizontal and the vertical. This is the centre of our being, the place where our self-giving is rooted in the sacrifice of Christ on the cross. The heart opens to love, fulfilling the divine will in which heaven and earth meet and embrace.

5. *Father, give us this day our daily bread (solar plexus)*

So we come to the place where we were nourished before we were born and where we now meet with the Bread of life which feeds and transfigures us. This is the seed of life, gradually making our body spiritual, of the Spirit. Here the inner self is renewed day after day.

6. *Father, forgive us our trespasses as we forgive those who trespass against us (bowels)*

Here are reflected those attitudes which I have when I am confronted by myself, by others, by the world and by God. Here they all flow together. Pride and possessiveness make us slaves, blind and withdrawn from communion, human, cosmic and divine. Love, though, opens us up and transforms our being into gift, so that even that sensuality which is so deeply inscribed in our human essence, is made free and drawn towards the highest goals. The Lord renews a spirit of holiness even in our guts. There we can be reclothed in deep feelings (the literal meaning of "viscera") of mercy, goodwill, humility, meekness, magnanimity, tolerance, forgiveness, charity, peace and gratitude (cf Col 3:12-15).

7. *Father, lead us not into temptation, but deliver us from evil (womb of life)*

We have now reached the root, the basal zone, down among the roots of our selves and here we gather together all generations, past and to come, and the earth itself from which we have arisen and by which we are nourished. This centre is the highest in the animals and the lowest in the human being. It follows that this always has the function of distancing us from the instinctual-animal level which is closed in on itself. This is so that we can reach up towards God with all those vital energies which have come to us from the Risen One. Reborn into the life of the Spirit, we have finally withdrawn from the dominion of the Evil One.

Our new thrust upwards is imaged by the cross which reaches heavenwards from the earth and stretches sideways to the boundaries of the whole world. This movement accompanies the concluding expression: "For yours is the kingdom..."

OUR FATHER
FROM THE OLD TO THE NEW TESTAMENT

In our private recitation of the Our Father, it will prove helpful to do as we do each time we proclaim the Gospel. That is, to precede our prayer by making the triple sign of the cross, once on the forehead, once on the lips and once on the breast. The Our Father, as Tertullian described it, is the *"compendium of the Gospel"*.[6] It is as if we are able, through this prayer, to incarnate the whole message of Christ. At the same time, we are being taught how this prayer, which Jesus himself gave his disciples, is to be rooted in the most important of our centres of energy. This prayer will energize those centres and flood them with the regenerating and transforming power of the Word. Nor should we forget the "sacramental" character which is traditionally seen in the Our Father, nor the way in which its words fill the one who says them.

In this prayer, then, we can gather all the fullness of the revelation from the Old and the New Testaments. The first three invocations underline the name, the kingdom and the divine will, all key issues in the theology of the chosen people. On Sinai, the revelation of the Name showed the transcendence and the historical reality of God. The people of the Covenant are a royal people. Fidelity to the Covenant means obedience to the commandments impressed on the two tablets of the Mosaic law.

Marked by sin and death, sacred history begins with the coming of the Messiah and the celebration of the paschal mystery. This is summed up in three supreme moments: the last supper, the crucifixion and descent into hell where death was overcome, sin destroyed and the gates of life opened again. It is quite possible to transform the Our Father into a daily memorial of this saving event, linking the last three invocations to Maundy Thursday, Good Friday and Holy Saturday[7]. Nor must we forget the words of Saint Teresa of Jesus which we have already quoted: "It is better to say a single word of the Our Father from time to time, than frequently to rush through the whole prayer".[8]

We would like to end on this note. We would like to underline our hope that these pages will offer support, not only in reciting the Our Father but in the whole practice of religion. We hope it will offer a more self-aware way of praying and living, with the result that they become more deeply satisfying and more effective.

NOTES TO PART FIVE

1. Anonimo, *Lo joga cristiano. La preghiera esicasta*, ed. G. Vannucci, Florence 1978, pp. 17-20: "The subtle centres in the Christian tradition" (with some adaptations). For a treatment of these centres in Christian monasticism, cf A. Bloom, *Asceticism: Somatopsychic techniques*, London 1957, n. 95 and 12-20. For the oriental tradition, cf Paramahansa Satyananda, *I Chakra*, Turin 1987; Maha Babaij (G. Furlan), *Condotti e centri supersottili*, Rome 1993. To find a universal basis, we need a "mystical physiology" leading to a reconsideration among Christians in order to align it with biblical and mystical tradition. On this, cf A. Gentili, *Organi psico-fisici*, in DES, 2, 1770ff.

2. The seven more important vital centres, superior or inferior, of which we have spoken, are rooted in the "subtle body" mentioned in the preceding pages. There are physical correspondents to these in the endocrine glands: the lowest centre/supra-renal; sacral/gonads; solar plexus/pancreas; heart/thymus; laringeal-pharungeal/thyroid; frontal/hypothalamus and pituitary; coronal/pineal and epithalamus. These centres of energy are like "doorways" through which the human organism absorbs and transmits cosmic energies and vital forces called *prana*. Finally, for each of these centres, which Asian physiology calls *chakras* or wheels corresponds a colour of the spectrum. According to a widespread understanding, the lowest centre, the coccyx/yellow; sacral/orange; solar plexus/red; heart/green; throat/blue; forhead/indigo and, at the top of the head, violet. The human "subtle body" is therefore revealed as a receptacle and fount of energy and light. This gather us into a mandala, as it were, composed of this aura in which all the spiritual forces which burst forth from us, are reflected. Such an aura is particularly evident with the saints.

3. S. Zedda, *Luke 1:35b; "Colui che nascerà santo, sarà chiamato Figlio di Dio"*, in "Rivista Biblica" 33 (1985) 29-43; 165-189.

4. *De resurrectione carnis*, 8: PL 2, 853.

5. The names given to the seven centres (*chakra*) in Asian mystical physiology are: *sahasrara, ajna, vishudda, anahata, manipura, svadhisthana, muladhara*. These mean, respectively: corona, centre of command, purity, inner sound, city of jewels, vital energy, root. There is an application of the vital centres or *chakra* to the Our Father, in: A. Bittlinger, *Das Vaterunser. Erlebt im Licht von Tiefenpsychologie und Chakrenmeditation*, Munich 1990.

6. Tertullian, *De oratione Domini*, 1,6: PL 1, 1153.

7. These are the essential biblical references: *Father:* Is 63:16; 64:7 ("For you are our father"); *Name:* Ex 3:12-15 ("I am who I am"); Judges 13:18 ("My name is wonderful"); Jer 15:16 ("I am called by your name"); Dt 28:10 ("All the peoples of the earth shall see that you are called by the name of the Lord"); *Kingdom:* Ex 19:6 ("You shall be for me a kingdom ..."); *Will:* Ex 20:1ff and Dt 5:1ff (about the Decalogue and the Torah in general); Ex 19:8.

8. Teresa of Jesus, *The Way of Perfection*, 31, 31.

Appendix

THE OUR FATHER AND ITS JEWISH SOURCES

In the Old Testament there are a multitude of texts to parallel each invocation of the Our Father and the key words of the Lord's Prayer. It seems in line with our approach to make some reference to the Jewish tradition. "In general, one can say that there is nothing in the Our Father which we do not find in various Jewish prayers, but that nothing in them is in any way comparable to the prayer of Jesus. In particular, we must compare the Our Father with two of the greatest prayers of Judaism: the *Quaddish* and *The Eighteen Blessings (shemoneh 'esreh)*."[1]

This is the scheme of *The Eighteen Blessings*:

> 3 benedictions in praise of God,
> 12 benedictions of petition,
> 3 benedictions of thanksgiving.

The Our Father grew out of this scheme, which is why the first Christians added: "For yours is the kingdom, the power and the glory, now and forever. Amen".[2] *The Eighteen Blessings* is too long to set out here, apart from that of *Quaddish*, which is as follows:

> May his great name be magnified and holy in the world which he has created according to his will.
> May his kingdom come during your lifetime and in your days, and during the lifetime of the whole house of Israel, in a short while and soon.
> *R.* Amen.

May his great Name be blessed for ever and ever.
May the Name of the Holy One be praised, glorified, exalted and celebrated. May he be blessed who pronounces this Name in the world.
R. Amen.

May heaven grant great peace and prosperity to us and to Israel.
R. Amen.

May he who establishes peace in high places, in his mercy establish peace upon us and upon Israel.
R. Amen.

Blessed be the Lord, worthy of praise.
Blessed be the Lord, worthy of praise in eternity and forever.
R. Amen.

Other minor texts, although no less significant, are:

"Our Father in heaven, may your Name be praised for all eternity" (*Seder Elijah*).

"Now his kingdom will be revealed to every creature" (*The Assumption of Moses*).

"May your will be done, in heaven, on high, and give tranquil courage to those upon earth who live in fear" (*R. Eliezer*).

"Our Father, our King, forgive and remit all our faults. Cast far away and cancel the sins we have committed in your sight" (*Abinu Mal-kenu*).

"See our affliction, sustain our cause and set us free for your Name's sake" (*Ghe'ullah,* n. 22).[3]

NOTES TO APPENDIX

1. P. Stefani, *Il Padre nostro*, Genoa 1991, p. 31.
2. *Didache*, 8, 2.
3. Cf C. Di Sante, *La preghiera di Israele*, Casale Monferrato 1980, pp. 21-24; M. Cunz (ed.) *Tradizione rabbinica e Nuovo Testamento*, in "Vita Monastica" 38 (1984) 85-91. Cf too: E. Lodi, *Liturgia della Chiesa*, Bologna 1981, p. 475; Schalom Ben-Chorim *Fratello Gesù. Un punto di vista ebraico sul Nazareno*, Brescia 1985, esp. the chapter: *Insegnaci a pregare*, pp. 150-161.